Reasons For
HAUNTINGS

A Step By Step Guide
To Understanding Haunted Places

By Rick Hayes

Stellium Books
Grant Park, Illinois 60940

i

About The Author

Rick Hayes
Psychic Medium/Life Consultant

"Amazing and very real - The best at what he does"
Christopher Saint Booth – Producer/Director Spooked
Productions

Rick Hayes is a longtime friend and very gifted. His
insights have brought comfort to many people over the
years. "Reasons For Hauntings" is a well written book full
of such help and insights.

2013 and 2014 Psychic Medium of the Year –
Paranormal Awards Association

A Top 50 Psychic in America

"Top 100 Psychics and Astrologers in America"
2014 book by Paulette Cooper and Paul Noble

Rick Hayes is the founder of LifesGift, Inc. – an association that supports his consultation and speaking engagement services. As a psychic medium and life consultant with unique abilities, Rick consults on a daily basis with those that have questions on life and the life-after.

As a speaker and lecturer, Rick has shared his unique insight with inspiration and enthusiasm to thousands since 2003. Rick's speaking invitations range from a small organization group to major events and conventions attended by thousands. Rick's wide range of topics is designed to accommodate each speaking invitation.

As a published and best-selling author, Rick's books include 'Stepping Stones –Thoughts Along Life's Path' (ISBN# 978-0-9765434-3-5) and 'You're not Crazy, You Have A Ghost' (ISBN#978-0-0965434-2-8). Rick's articles appear on numerous print and online publications.

Rick is a media favorite appearing on television, film, radio, and print media including appearances on The Travel Channel, SYFY Network, Chiller Channel, Fox Television, CBS Radio, and Sirius Satellite Radio.

Rick is featured in the docu-film 'The Possessed' (NBC Universal/Spooked Productions) and 'Soul Catcher' (NBC Universal/Spooked Productions) on the SYFY Television Network. Rick also appears on the Travel Channel's 'Most Terrifying Places In America' and 'Children of The Grave 2' (NBC/Chiller Network).

Contents

BElieve...

Could A Place Really Be Haunted?

"I know I saw someone walking down the stairs, but she had a ghostly appearance! I believe she may be a trapped spirit. I am not sure how to reason this whole experience."

"Can You Learn To Understand Haunted Places?"

YES YOU CAN!

Now Appearing At A Location Near You!

"Don't go there! The place is haunted with ghosts and everything!"

How many times in your life heard about a 'home that has ghosts' or 'the dead still walks in that location'? Did you feel a combination of emotions that included fear with curiosity, mixed with maybe a little bit of non-belief? You were a little bit afraid, but also said "I would love to check the place out!"

Today the thought of a haunting is mainstream in the media. On practically every television channel, you can find a documentary of an eerie location, organizations 'ghost hunting', and sitcoms that include 'the energy of the life after' as their backdrop. Hundreds of radio shows air their main subject as paranormal or supernatural.

Newspapers, magazines, and the internet include pages of 'a haunted experience.'

So what about hauntings? Are they real or a figment of imagination? Do ghosts or energies of the life after actually remain in a place?

Could they be trapped there, and why do they remain if they are not trapped? Are they out to 'get you' if you invade their space? Do they want to be noticed for a reason when they are caught on tape?

Haunt A Definition

Let start by looking at the word -haunt. Often we perceive the word as 'a place where ghosts are'. How many times have you visited a commercial 'haunted house' during Halloween and anticipated to 'screaming a little' because you knew it was going to have scary things inside. Admit it; you let out a scream as you inched your way through holding to your friends while the 'ghosts and goblins' popped out!

The word haunt (Webster's New Ideal Dictionary) definition is "to visit often, to continually seek the company of, to stay around or persist". The definition's final statement expresses, "to visit or inhabit - as a ghost.'

Therefore, in a sense, we actually 'haunt' or own home. As I look around my home, I conclude "well what do you know - I am in a haunted house! I visit here often; I enjoy being the company within the home. I live or inhabit here."
"I must be a ghost!"

BElieve...

Construction Zone
Location-Location-Location

Ok, let us get down to the nuts and bolts. We will start at the location of a haunted place. To learn about haunted places can be in comparison to building a house. You begin by where the location of your new home is to be constructed. Therefore, we begin understanding the reason for the haunted place by looking at the location.

Write down a haunted location that you have visited or you know of in the space below. This may be your own home (just like Karen's in our book 'You're Not Crazy, You Have A Ghost') or it may be a home that you have visited (like the Myrtle Plantation). The location may be famous such as the Waverly Hills Sanatorium or Gettysburg Cemetery. It is best if you write down a place that you have had a personal experience of visiting - but if not simply write the name of a place that you know.

The Name of the Haunted Place is:

_____

Next, in the following spaces below, add the reasons why you believe this place is haunted. It may be from the stories you have heard or personal experiences.

Why I Believe This Place Is Haunted

Historic Reasons

_____

_____

_____

_____

Personal Reasons

_____

_____

_____

_____

Now back to our 'haunted house building scenario'. To build a house it is best if you know as much as possible about the land you are building your house on.

I remember when I built my first home. I painstakingly researched for the right place, my builders made sure the ground was suitable for building, and we would be happy there upon completion.

It is the same for understanding haunted places. You should research the history of the land. A location is full of past memories and experiences. The location may have included a residence of a teepee, a log home, and/or a mansion. Take a moment to think about your own home or current residence. Do you know anything about the land's history that your home is setting on?

Although you may believe you are the only ones who resided on the land, it has experiences and memories for those who have moved on.

Below you will find recommendations to begin researching the history of your current residential land. The more you know - the more you grow!

Research Tools

- **Local Library** - *Genealogical and/or community history section*

- **City/County Court Records** - *County record research is recommended*

- **Local Historical Society** - *Schedule an appointment*

- **Person-to-Person Research** - *Research the family tree of the location and schedule to meet a family member. (State that you are researching the location, most often they are more than happy to meet with you. Older members of the community may also have memories of the location that will be helpful. If the location is your own residence, research your own family history)*

- **Internet** - *search terms include the name of the location, person, or address of location*

Construction Zone
Solid Foundation

Ok, now we move to the next step - the foundation. A foundation is a structure that is a creation for support. So what is the foundation to create the support of a haunted location?

Three Words Experiences, Memories, and Understanding.

So very often, we tend to allow the emotion of 'fear' to create 'a haunted feeling'.

Why?

We simply fear what we do not understand. Each one of us has something that we are afraid of. It is funny, ghosts never really bother me, but I tend to be frightened by something as natural as a snake.

I have chosen not to understand the background of a snake. It may sound weird - but I have been around 'ghosts' throughout my life and this does not bother me, but have a snake cross my path and I jump higher than a pro basketball player!

On the spaces below, write down the three things that you fear the most. This could be something such as fear of heights, fear of ghosts, to even the number one fear - the fear of death itself.

My Three Fears

_____

_____

_____

Next, write below what brought on this fear, such as a past experience.

Why I Fear My Top Three

Fear #1

_____

_____

_____

_____

_____

_____

Fear #2

_____

_____

_____

_____

_____

_____

Fear #3

_____

_____

_____

_____

_____

_____

In my book 'You're Not Crazy, You Have A Ghost', I wrote the following statement in regards to haunted places.

"The only thing to fear is fear itself - but to understand will eliminate the fear"

Think about that statement for a moment. Why do we become frightened by what we may be told is a haunted place? Is it truly because we do not fully understand what we do not know?

Do we really know anything about the afterlife? Have you ever heard the phrase:

"You won't know until you're there"?

I believe when we receive 'signs' from loved ones in spirit who have moved on, it is not to say

"We are haunting you and this place" But rather...

"We are here and we want to help you better understand".

I feel so often we misinterpret the supernatural life. We really cannot blame our own selves. We grew up with movies and television shows showing us to 'fear' the unknown, or what we may have heard from adults while growing up. To state it as blunt as I can - scary things sell tickets.

If we change our mindset to understanding that the life after is simply a part of life, it becomes less frightening.

Look at it this way. Write down the name of a person you love the most that is still living in their earthly path in the space below.

The One I Love Still Walking With Me In My Life Path Is:

_____

Say that you have completed your plan and now a part of the 'afterlife' - or if you wish to be defined as such, a ghost.

Would you, if you knew you were given the ability to be around them, attempt the following?

- Show them you are ok?
- Show them you are still with them?
- Guide them along their path in life?
- Show them that there is nothing to be afraid of?

So why would your answer be different from those who have moved on, or maybe I should use the word 'ghosts'?

Would they not answer the same as you and me?

You see, I feel that often when we believe a place is 'haunted'; it is simply loved ones who have moved on trying to show us they are ok. To let us know they are still around, and to share with us experiences and memories to guide us better in life. They are attempting to get our attention without frightening us - so that we better understand the location.

When we receive a validation of some kind - they are acknowledging their presence for us to know that life is continual.

BElieve...

Construction Zone
Trap Door

You may be thinking what many believe that spirits in these places are actually 'trapped' due to how they were in their earthly path, missing a piece of a puzzle in their earthly life, or simply was 'taken suddenly' by an unforeseen occurrence at the particular location.

Write on the space below an occurrence that made you personally feel physically trapped.

I remember having the feeling of being physically trapped when:

_____

_____

_____

_____

_____

_____

I recall an experience of which I was stuck in an elevator for several minutes. I honestly did not feel I was ever going to get out!

Next to your experience, write in the space below how you felt when you were trapped, and how you became 'untrapped' (is that a word?).

During this experience, I felt:

_____

_____

_____

_____

_____

_____

I was able to 'un-trap' myself by:

_____

_____

_____

_____

_____

_____

Your experience of entrapment occurred when you were in a physical body. Unlike the amazing spiritual energy within, your physical body is restricted to certain conditions.

In a personal elevator experience, I physically continued to push the buttons with my fingers, looked around for an escape with my eyes, listened and felt for any sounds of movement from the elevator itself. My physical body is restricted to physical traits.

So what about a spiritual energy when one moves on?

Simply, it does not have a restriction from earthly boundaries - but freedom through spiritual energy.

Often we hear how ghosts are documented to 'walk through walls' in a location, and I often wonder

"So, they are able to walk through walls, but they cannot escape a place or location?"

I do not feel our loved ones are trapped in a location. Try this. Look around your home right now - how long have you been there? Now think about all of the memories and experiences you have created there. You have many don't you - some make you smile, others make you sad, and others may bring you contentment. If you would ever move from your current residence, you would always have those memories and experiences to share with others.

Remember the home where you grew up? Do you recall the memories like they were yesterday - and if you had the opportunity to visit your childhood home - would you be able to share with those now living in your home those memories?

I feel it is the same for our loved ones in spirit who have moved on. They are given the gift of loving memories and experiences they had while in their own earthly plan.

When we visit their 'residence of memories and experiences', they are simply there to share with us 'what it was like'. Just like you visiting your childhood home or someone visiting with you at your residence now, the loved ones who have moved on in spirit are sharing with us "back when I lived here" - but leave when we leave and are around those they love."

BElieve...

Reasons For Hauntings

<u>Construction Zone</u>
<u>Moving In</u>

We are now ready to add the walls, roof, and the unique form of our house. We set up the walls of our house to create rooms that provide the sense of comfort, protection, uniqueness, and purpose. The roof protects us from elements of the earth, and the unique form of the house gives us the feeling of 'this is my house'.

It is the same when we consider a haunted place. At one time, the haunted place was a residence of a loved one.

What we look at as 'haunted', were walls of comfort, protection, uniqueness, and purpose for a loved one in spirit who had moved on. It is a place that our loved ones in spirit guide our experience while visiting the physical elements of the earth, a unique form that relays to us "this is their house".

'Ghosts' or energies are not captured by us 'seeing them' with our physical eyes, cameras, or audio tapes. They are not standing there saying, "Oops, you caught me" - but rather saying "here I want to validate I am here". We must understand that they know best when we are to acknowledge them and know the reason why better than we do. This is why you may visit a place and not receive any validations, and other times you may.

Here is something I would recommend. Take out your boxes or albums of old family pictures. Re-examine them to see if there may be a 'validation' within the picture.
Now be careful - sometimes it may be bad film, a dust particle, or a logical reason. However, you may also have a validation within the photo in which the loved one said, "Hey - I would like to be in this picture!" If you're not sure, email the photo to us and I will assist.

Once we begin to understand the reasons for 'Haunted Places', we will understand that the 'haunted house' is just a 'home'. A home is a house that has been filled with memories, experiences, family embraces, happiness, and challenges, among others.

The 'Haunted' - becomes 'Home.'

BElieve...

Reasons For Hauntings

Comfort Zone
Summary Highlights

You have completed your 'understanding of a haunted place' and thinking, "Well this sure did take some of the excitement away from haunted places!"

The excitement is still there, but it is now added with a dose of comfort. The steps you have just read should build your excitement to learn more about haunted places and life-after. You will enter places with a renewal of vision and a reduction of inner fear, and will receive a growth in experience and understanding.

Remember, the gift of life creates a purpose - to build experiences, memories, and everlasting spirit. What you create today - will be lessons for generations to come.

- **Haunt:** "to visit often, to continually seek the company of, to stay around or persist. To visit or inhabit - as a ghost".

- **Research** the history of the land to learn from past memories and experiences.
  The support structure of a haunted location

- **Experiences** - Memories - and Understanding "The only thing to fear is fear itself - but to understand will eliminate the fear"

- **Change your mindset** to understand that the life after is simply a part of life.

- **A validation** - The acknowledgment of presence for us to know that life is everlasting.

- **Spirits do not have a restriction from earthly boundaries** - but freedom through spiritual energy.

- **When we visit their 'residence of memories and experiences',** they are simply there to share with us 'what it was like.'

- **A haunted place** was at one time a residence for a loved one.

- **They know best** when we are to acknowledge them and know the reason why better than we do.

BElieve...

Reasons For Hauntings

"Why Are They Still Here?"

"This place has a history and been abandoned for many years, so why do we hear strange sounds and see eerie entities?"

"Do they not want us to be here?"

The History Is The Clue!

A Piece Of History

At the beginning of earth's creation, the birth of historic experiences and places begin with immediate compassion. History can be found in every walk of life, through each portal of time. History feeds on the moments of time, and leaves behind a never forgotten memory.

Throughout the time of life, structures built by man include history within the walls, land, and sea. The walls of a historic home or building include memories of long ago. Locations where a significant piece of the past of a historic occurrence, such as a battle between differences include memories that are never to be forgotten. The earth's waters where a ship filled with lost souls include a part of history. History can be found at each step in life.

There are those that believe these historic locations also include something 'beyond our earthly life'. Certain locations of history have been given the definition of being a 'Haunted Place'. The question is

"Could a historic place actually be haunted?"

Just as we shared together in the first section, we will learn with each step a better understanding on if historic places can be filled with 'ghostly spirits' and if so why they are 'inhabiting the history'.

BElieve...

In The Beginning

So what about historic haunted places? Are they real or a figment of imagination? Do ghosts or energies of the life after actually remain in a historic place for a specific reason? Could they be historically trapped, and why do they remain if they are not trapped? Are they remaining as a residual piece of history, and do they have a message of importance?

We begin understanding the history of the location, more specifically where it all began - at the beginning.

Begin by writing below the name of a historic place that you have personally visited. For me, there are many – including President's homes, hotels, southern mansions, Navy ships, and military forts, just to name a few.

The Historic Place I Remember Visiting Is:

_____

_____

How much do you truly know about this historic location? More specifically, do you know why the location was originally built? Does it include in its history more than one purpose?

A famous hotel built in the late 1800's is rich in history. Today it is still utilized as a thriving hotel filled with hospitality, but with research, we find it has been many other purposes along its historic path. Originally built as a resort for the rich, it later became a hospital, a girl's school, and today a hotel. The hotel is well known to house 'spirits walking the halls'.

It is important to know the complete history of a location to understand the 'ghosts' within. The 'ghosts' within the hotel mentioned above- are a part of the different historic eras of the hotel. If you visited or investigated the hotel and only knew the location as an 'old and famous hotel', you may miss the actual understanding of the spirit's presence.

<u>Research Findings</u>

List any information that you have discovered from doing research on your location.

_____

_____

_____

_____

_____

_____

_____

_____

_____

_____

_____

_____

_____

_____

_____

_____

_____

_____

_____

_____

_____

_____

_____

_____

_____

_____

_____

_____

_____

_____

_____

The Middle

Within the paranormal industry, words of definition are targeted to specify certain criteria. As you browse through a book of paranormal, you may find words such as:

- **Anomaly:** something strange or unusual

- **Apparition:** a ghostly figure

- **EVP:** Electronic Voice Phenomenon

- **Ghost:** a disembodied soul

- **Residual:** a spirit trapped within a certain experience in their earthly life and replays the experience over and over.

- **Spirit Guide:** an advanced soul who assists with the life of one who is still in earthly life.

With the majority of historic locations, any or all of the words above have been used by those who have experienced or investigated the particular location.

So why should we identify or even assume a paranormal presence within a paranormal location?

It can all be described in 4 words: Historic Memories - Historic Experiences

You see, every location created includes selected and structured experiences for that location. Everlasting memories are therefore created through these selected experiences.

Let us go back to the historic hotel mentioned earlier. The hotel began as a memorable resort for travelers. With each individual who included an experience of staying at the hotel, this created an unforgettable memory for that particular individual. Those who were employed at the hotel added to their life path daily experiences, with unforgettable daily routines. Upon the hotel being transformed into a hospital, the doctors, nurses, and patients created new experiences with memories.

Basically stated, the reason for a historical place to be 'haunted' can be defined as a place that was a part of a loved one's {ghosts) memories and experiences. Who better to know and share what it was like within the location than those who were there and absolutely knows the place better than anyone?

I love sharing this thought when asked to be a part of a historic location investigation:

"They are here as tour guides to show us what it was truly like during this time and place. When we leave, they leave."

Do I ever receive a jaw drop on that statement! Many believe that ghosts are trapped as a residual, or for an experience in their life they must remain in. When I make such as bold statement as 'they leave when we leave', there are those who ask with disagreement

'How can you explain this?"

Answer: "They are no longer restricted to their earthly bodies"

Let us think about this for a moment. If something is in a concrete form {such as your physical body), it is restricted to certain conditions. Your physical body cannot walk through walls, be in two places at the same time, or change shape {unless plastic surgery is involved).

A spiritual body is just that - a body of energy or spirit. It is not restricted to earthly conditions.

Apparently, the spirit of the body is an energy we are each created with to inhibit after the death of our physical body. It has the capabilities we are yet to fully understand, but do know it is not restricted to the physical body.

So to say a spiritual energy {ghost) is confined to a specific location or experience is hard for me to swallow. If a ghost has the ability {as it has been documented) to transform through walls - what would stop them from being any place they choose?

Aha - did you happen to catch that last word? Choose.

Along our daily life, we are given a gift – the ability to make our own choices. We choose how we feel, the environment, dreams and goals, and experiences.

In the afterlife - the gift of choice is still with us. Ghosts choose to be in a location, choose to be around those they wish to guide, and choose to share what they have learned about life.

"Ghosts {loved ones) chose to be in the location to share their experiences and memories with us - not to harm us or bring fear to us - but to guide us in understanding completely the location's historic memories."

The End
{And you are beginning)

Although this may be the end of Reasons for Hauntings - Other Places Other Experiences, it is actually the beginning for you!

- Begin by opening your inner mind with new doors of possible opportunities - Believe and You Will Receive!

- Begin with the understanding that all places that are historic are filled in abundance for your to learn about life in the past {ahem - past lives).

- Begin by not accepting the thought of fear - to understand will eliminate the fear

- Begin by creating a renewed outlook on what may be, what could be - will be

- Begin to visit the historic places with a new outlook

- You have 'spiritual tour guides' to assist you. BEGIN - RIGHT NOW!

Other Books by Rick Hayes

'You're Not Crazy, You Have A Ghost'
by Rick Hayes and K. Coons
Revised Edition 2015
Stellium Books

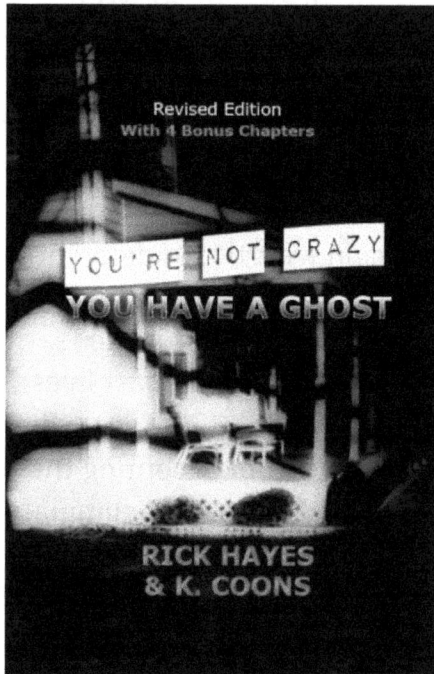

"A Great Guide to Ghosts and More"
Jordan Rich – Host WBZ Radio Boston
"Very Easy To Follow Workbook"
P.Wheelock – Editor in Chief Beyond Investigation Magazine
"A Most Unique Book"
Sandman – Host Parareality Radio

Stepping Stones
Thoughts Along Life's Path
Second Edition 2015
Stellium Books

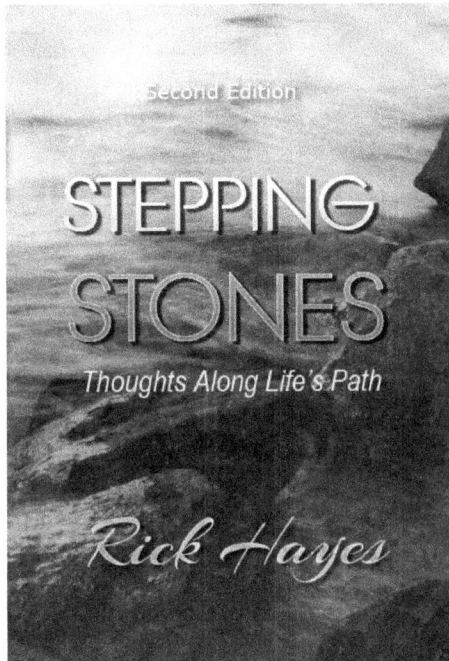

Psychic medium Rick Hayes shares his inspirational thoughts for personal growth and a richer life. Written with profound sincerity, the inspirational book Stepping Stones - Thoughts Along Life's Path captures in-depth thoughts on subjects including: Life after Death, The Reasons for Trials in Life, Reincarnation, The Gift of Family, and The Evolution Theory.

Amazing Paranormal Encounters
Volume 2
Stellium Books 2016

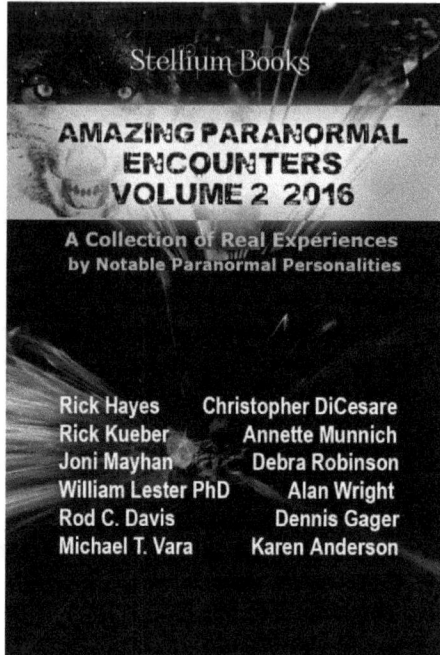

The follow-up book to the top 20 best seller in Supernatural and Unexplained Mysteries on Amazon since October 2015 AMAZING PARANORMAL ENCOUNTERS VOLUME 1. Bone-chilling tales of ghosts and more written by authors, investigators, radio show hosts and other people in the paranormal field. This chilling anthology reveals some of the strangest and most frightening experiences they have ever had and in some cases, these experiences are what brought them into the field of the paranormal in the beginning. Contains links to EVP's.

www.ingramcontent.com/pod-product-compliance
Lightning Source LLC
Chambersburg PA
CBHW071745020426
42331CB00008B/2187